I0505641

BUSINESS PLAN WRITING

HOW TO WRITE AN IMPRESSIVE BUSINESS PLAN FOR YOUR STARTUP BUSINESS OR COMPANY

By

METE CAN YUMRU

Copyright © 2015 Mete Can Yumru

All Rights Reserved

ISBN#: 978-1508803324

PREFACE

Whether you are planning to start your own business as a sole proprietor, take on partners and form a limited liability company, or incorporate to form a public company, there is one thing that will make your business run smoothly and will provide you with a significant advantage in the long run. What you need is **a business plan.**

A business plan is the **foundation** of your business. It is the one document everyone needs to write extremely well not only because they feel obliged to impress investors, managers, and customers alike, but because it will serve as a guide for the business.

As your business shapes and grows, you can compare the projected business in your business plan with your actual one. It will show you how well you have looked into **the future**, and how much the reality of **the present** differed from your initial vision. Shortcomings, financial forecasts, unforeseen events; everything is based on a professionally formed and accurate business plan.

My first experience with writing a business plan in a very serious manner was for a group project for my Entrepreneurship and Innovation module that I have taken last year at Durham University, UK. We were 6 students who worked as a team to come up with an idea and make it into a real business, hot from the oven, **ready** to go. I loved this experience because it taught me the importance of creating a business plan and more importantly how to write a **really good** business plan.

Now, as an aspiring businessman waiting to start my own design business, I have written my **very own** business plan. However, I realized that while it is always exciting to venture down the entrepreneur path, the process of writing a business plan can be very taxing and often confusing to say the least. Considering the abundance of often conflicting information online, I found myself compelled to write about this topic. After all, when things started to get **serious**, I needed to get serious as well by thinking not only about how to write a good business plan but also whether what I wrote was **actually** going to work.

In short, I have written this book to lay out information on how to approach this important task and how to pull it off effectively with satisfying results, **without** paying to third parties so that you can minimize outsider intervention. Throughout this book, I will keep everything **simple** by putting all relevant information into helpful descriptions, bullet points, and examples to guide you through writing your very own business plan.

So here we go…

LEGAL NOTES

This book is for entertainment purposes only. The author is not responsible of any business decisions you make based on the ideas, concepts, experiences, information, and any other form of word transfer in this book. You (and you alone) are responsible for your success in business or otherwise.

The author is not responsible for any form of damage that this book really should not cause, whether it be in financial, psychological, physical, or in any other form. It is up to you to decide which information is useful to you and whether to use it or not while you write your business plan. I wrote this book with the best available information at hand at the time I wrote it, and do not guarantee the success of your business in terms of convincing angel investors, getting a bank loan, impress clients and in any way, shape or form.

This book is licensed for your personal enjoyment only. It may not be re-sold or given away to other people. If you would like to share this book with another person, please purchase an additional copy for each person you fancy to share it with.

Copyright © 2015 Mete Can Yumru.

All rights reserved. Including the right to reproduce this book or portions thereof, in any form. No part of this text may be reproduced in any form without the express written permission of the author.

TABLE OF CONTENTS

BUSINESS PLAN OUTLINE

Title Page

Identifies who you are.

Executive Summary

Tells the reader what you company is about.

Table of Contents

Lists the different sections.

Overview of the Business

This section describes in more detail what your business is and what demand it fulfils.

Marketing and Selling Product or Service

All information relating to selling your product or service such as your choice of pricing method, price calculations, survey questions, survey results and analysis (including important pie charts, bar charts, tables, etc.).

Making and Delivering Product or Service

Describe how you are planning on plan on creating and distributing a product or service.

Strategy

This includes your mission-vision-values, SWOT analysis, stakeholder map, and expansion and exit strategies.

The Team

Briefly explain who you are (and partners if applicable) and list your experiences.

Financial Analysis

This section shows your cost breakdowns and allows the reader to see how well you have planned in the future.

Legal Aspects and Sustainability

Legal and risk assessment matters and impact to the environment

References

Lists all external information sources.

Appendices

Lists all internal information sources.

CHAPTER 1: WHY WRITE A BUSINESS PLAN?

Before you start a business or a company, it is critical to write a well laid out business plan. Depending on the scope of the business and the amount of detail in the business plan, this might take a few weeks, however it definitely worth taking the time to write it.

A business plan will help you do the following:
- ✓ Define your business idea
- ✓ Set up short term and long term goals for your business
- ✓ Lists the capabilities of the firm
- ✓ Serves the purpose of validation
- ✓ Provides credentials of key people
- ✓ Underlines risks
- ✓ Serve as a roadmap for future decisions

Let's go into detail for these points before we start planning for and writing the actual business plan. The details in each section are important because they will underline why you should place specific information under specific sections and how to maximize the effectiveness of your business plan.

Define Your Business Idea

A business idea is exactly what it sounds like; an idea of what you want your business to be about and the basis for your business plan. A well thought out business idea will help you and all parties to get a clear picture of what the business does. These parties could be angel investors, employees of venture capital firms or banks, insurance companies, friends, family, or clients just to name a few. For ease of reading, these parties will be referred to as '**readers**' throughout the book.

When defining your business idea, you should be as clear and concise as you can. Always assume that you will be sending your business plan in the mail to a venture capital firm where there will be no presentation or follow-up for you to better explain your business, yet they will understand everything you have written.

This does not mean that you will have no communication with the people who read your business plan, but it is a good assumption to make so that there will be no questions in the mind of the reader. A good business idea speaks for itself. If you do not fully understand your own idea when you put it down on paper, assume that the reader will **not** understand it either.

Set Up Business Goals

Setting up business goals is all about asking yourself questions. What do you hope to achieve? **For example,** if you are starting a catering business, how many branches are you planning on having within the next year? How much revenue do you need for the business to keep running? By how much are you planning to exceed this goal?

Business goals can be **quantitative** or **qualitative**. Quantitative goals include everything that can be counted such as revenues, number of people that will be using your service or product, number of offices or employees you will have, possible reductions in costs without compromising quality (possibly by reducing costs of production by mass production or lean six sigma), etc. Everything that can be accounted for with a calculator is **quantitative**.

Qualitative is, as the name implies, about the quality of the product or service. In other words, how your business is **perceived** by your customers. Instead of accounting, the quality of a product or service can be measured by surveys or through evaluation by a respected independent third party (could be a private or government held entity) relevant to the business. This is why for most services, there will be a survey asking you to rate the service you received. This is an attempt by businesses to **quantify** how well they are achieving their **qualitative** goals so that they can offer the **best service** to their customers.

Quantitative goals are generally analysed or defined in the financial forecasts whereas the qualitative goals are laid out in the mission statement. There is no strict rule as to where to place these goals but it is better to include them where they will be more relevant.

List Capabilities

Capability is what the company can do with the resources it has (money, people facilities, etc.). A business plan will help you realize the capabilities and understand the limitations of your business so that you can better plan for future expansions and/or improvements. **For example,** if you are planning to rent a small factory for the production of a medical appliance, you need to estimate how many units you can produce per year based on the size of the factory, number of employees in the assembly line, and the start-up and operational costs of your business.

As a further example, you might say that "with 10 employees working the assembly line and with an initial budget of $50000, it is estimated that all of the operational costs (renting the factory, employee salaries, electricity, insurance, etc.) will be covered for the duration of only 3 months. Based on the calculations attached (place Appendix reference here), the factory will be able to produce 100 units/month."

This statement provides a clear picture of listing a **capability,** by stating how many units can be produced each month and how long the business can run without going into debt. Of course, this is a pessimistic scenario and assumes that no units will be sold for 3 months. However, I gave this example to illustrate the description of a capability.

Furthermore, having a competitive advantage for your business is a capability. That means asking yourself a few questions. What can you do that your competitors cannot? What makes your business idea special? Providing proof of this is a good idea, however if this information is sensitive or not patented you must always be careful how much detail you give the reader.

A Tool For Validation

Validation happens when you use an outside source to verify your own data. If you make a calculation that says you need to sell 100 units to stay in business, you must confirm it with data for it to be valid. The business plan is an **excellent** tool for validation because it will serve as a compilation of all information and calculations related the business. The information and analysis in your business plan can then be used for the following types of validation.

Financial Validation: You can validate that the company will be profitable and you will be able to make at least as much as your start-up costs as well as grow your business. Much of the work produced for this type of validation will be discussed in later sections, but here is essentially what you will do. You should calculate start-up costs using Excel as well as prepare a cash flow forecast (discussed in Chapter 4) if you did not start the business yet, and a cash flow statement if you have started the business. You should also prepare an income statement (also referred to as profit and loss statement). Additionally, you can prepare a balance sheet to show your company's assets and liabilities.

Design Validation: Design validation is used to prove that the function and specifications of a product are in line with the needs of the customer. If you were designing a medical ventilator device, the design validation can be done by conducting tests to see whether all functions of a prototype unit are working properly and whether the device is safe to use on patients. A design validation can also be done with a simulation instead of testing a working prototype. **For example,** using a process called Finite Element Analysis (a simulation) you can check how well a product can withstand heat or pressure.

Design validation is important depending on what your product does. **For example,** if you are designing a wind turbine, you need to make sure that the tower will be able to withstand the pressure of the spinning blades and be efficient enough to produce an optimal amount of energy.

Validation of Market Demand: You can achieve this type of validation by conducting surveys. I will talk about this more in Chapter 4. You are trying to prove here that your product **will** sell.

Validation of Competitive Advantage: This can also be verified by conducting a survey. It will show how much the competitor's products are selling and whether your product's special features or new way of delivering service will increase sales.

Validation of Logistics: This is when the location of your operations is very important to the success of your business. In this case you need to optimize the location of your facility and show proof that you have picked an ideal location.

It is important to note that for some types of businesses, certain types of validation may not be valid. As an example, for a business that provides a service, design validation may not be necessary.

Provide Credentials

Your business plan is an opportunity for you to summarize your credentials to the reader. Your credentials are your knowledge and experience of your success or interest related to the business. It is highly recommended to provide proof of your credentials so that your business plan will look more appealing to the reader. You may not have the experience for the particular business you start, but that does not mean you will fail. Rather, it means you will learn along the way. If this is the case, you can provide reasons that represent your strong belief of **why** you will succeed in the business. This may be anything from communication skills to managerial experience even though the skill may not be directly related to the type of business you will start.

You and your partners' credentials are the foundation that everything will be based upon. The more credentials you can provide, the better it will be for the persuasiveness of your business plan. If you have credentials that are relevant, well laid out, and backed with proof, the readers and stakeholders will be more easily persuaded to support you.

If you feel that you are lacking in credentials, there are always ways to give yourself more. **For example,** if you need more communication skills, you can attend or help plan a charity event. If you need more managerial skills, you can take on a new responsibility at your current job or at school.

Underline Risks

The business plan will help you draw emphasis on the risks your business will face. This is critical not only for stakeholders, but you and your business partners as well. Avoiding the risks your business will possibly face is not a good idea. Doing that would mean you turn a blind eye to reality and will have a harder time adjusting if things do not go the way you intended. Needless to say, it is a **fact** that during the span of any business from inception to liquidation, at least **something** will not go as planned. Doing business is all about quickly adapting to unforeseen events related to the reception of the product or service by the clients (in other words sales), problems with financing, issues related to human resources, competition, advertising, defects, legal aspects, and much more.

You might think that underlining the risks can be perceived negatively by the stakeholders or anyone who will read your business plan. However, knowing and clearly representing the risks in the business plan shows that you know what can go wrong and if it does, you know what to do about it. If people are convinced that you know the risks, your credibility can be increased dramatically. Do not to leave the main (or most critical) risks out, because if the reader thinks about an important risk that is not in your business plan, this might have a negative effect on the reader's opinion.

All information relating to the business is important in the business plan but I cannot stress enough about the importance of underlining risks. Unfortunately, the section underlining risks is often cut short or misinforms the reader to make the business plan sound more appealing. Do not cut it short, do not avoid it, and do not hide risks in fear of scaring the reader. If you intentionally do what I said not to do and show the finalized business plan to a venture capitalist or anyone who you seek funding from, they will know and discard your idea.

Serve As A Roadmap For Future Decisions

After you have finalized the business plan and have started your business, do not think that it is no longer useful. This is a document that will continually remind you how the business started and progressed. In fact, you can have newer versions of the business plan as important events come to fruition and keep it up to date by adding new goals.

The dangers of not following your business plan are that your business might get muddied and you might find yourself in places you didn't want to go. You may also lose control of the business because you may not be able to adjust to where your business is going.

By keeping the business plan handy and frequently referring to it, you can keep focused. Before you make a critical decision about your business, you can refer to the business plan and ensure that the new direction is feasible or improves the overall success of your business.

CHAPTER 2: THINGS TO KEEP IN MIND WHILE WRITING

This chapter focuses on what you need to think about even before you begin writing. If you follow my suggestions, you can save a lot of time while you are checking and editing your business plan later on. The key here is that you keep the readers' attention until the end of the plan, which will boost the chances that they will like it and support your business. After all, if they cannot stand reading it all the way through, it is highly unlikely that they will consider it seriously.

Doing the following will be useful to accomplish this:

- ✓ Make Use of Bullet Points
- ✓ Use Visual Aids
- ✓ Make It Concise
- ✓ Make All Relevant Information Available
- ✓ Be Realistic, Write Optimistically
- ✓ What Else to Avoid

If you follow these tips you can prepare an effective business plan as well as keep the readers' attention throughout.

Make Use of Bullet Points

Long paragraphs can lead to the reader getting lost in the text and easily losing focus. As you write, you might come to the realization that the text you wrote is becoming too bloated or complex. Breaking important information into bullet points will help the reader keep track of all of the information.

Whenever you have more than one concept, idea, or result that serves the same purpose or belongs to the same category, use bullet points. For example, when you are talking about the competitive advantage of your business, you might say:

"The business (or the Company XYZ) boasts various competitive advantages which can be summarized as follows but not limited to:

1-) Advantage 1

2-) Advantage 2

3-) Advantage 3"

Brilliant!! Now the reader can follow what you want to say easily and you have increased their attention span by giving them organized information.

Examples of where you can use bullet points are:

✓ To lay out the main results of the entire business plan in the executive summary section.
✓ To list just about anything in an organized manner such as competitive advantages, design specs, business goals, risk assessment, financial scenarios (optimistic, pessimistic), etc.

I recommend having bullet points in each chapter of your business plan. This is not required for it but if your business plan is detailed enough, you will see a need them anyways.

Use Visual Aids

Another way to ensure the business plan impresses the reader is to use visual aids. Some of these visual aids you may want to leave in the appendices if you think they would not add much to or clutter up the main body of the business plan. However, you should include them when you can.

Examples of visual aids that are helpful to prove a point or emphasize what you are talking about are:

Tables: Tables are great tools to represent important information in an organized manner. **For example,** if you want to show the specifications of your product with lots of important numbers, tables are a much better option than using sentences. This way you will not confuse the readers by representing these specifications (length, width, height, color, function, etc.) in an easy to follow format. You can use tables to compare your products if you have more than one as well.

Here is an example of how you can use a table to show the costs of different scenarios.

Cost Comparison Table ($)	ORIGINAL SCENARIO	ALTERNATIVE 1	ALTERNATIVE 2
Product Design	5000	2000	3000
Legal	2000	2000	2000
Insurance	1500	1500	1500
Salaries	1000	500	0
Accountancy	900	900	900
Other Expenses	500	500	200
Advertisement and Stationary	300	300	50
Telephone	200	200	400
Total	11300	7400	8050

In the table above, the original cost is compared to 2 alternatives that could reduce operational costs.

Charts: Charts are very useful to show cost distributions, survey result percentages, etc. For your start-up costs, it is very helpful to put a chart in your business plan to show what product or service will take up the most of the overall cost, and discuss what you can do to reduce it. Rather than saying salaries will cost 30%, equipment 20%, and other services will take up the rest, simply place a chart instead. There are many different kinds of charts but the ones most commonly used are pie charts, Pareto charts, and bar charts. Use a pie chart if you have a maximum of 10 different costs, if you have more you should consider using a Pareto chart because too many percentages on a pie chart can make it difficult to read.

Monthly Expenses

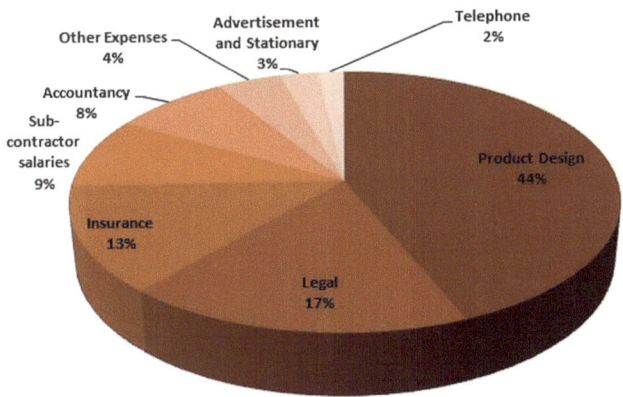

The 3-d pie chart above shows the monthly expense distribution. Alternatively we could have used a bar chart with the same data.

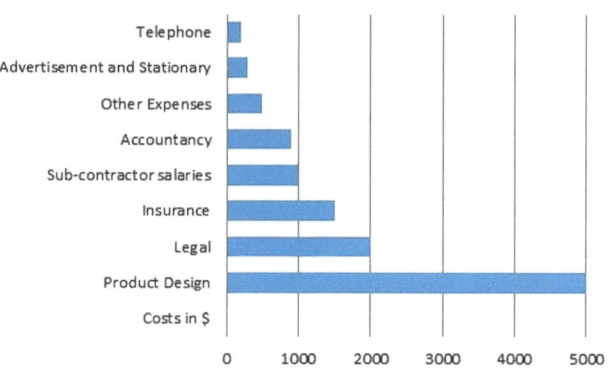

Monthly Expenses

Above is a 2-D bar chart created in Excel using the same data.

Plots: Plots are especially helpful to represent the results of experiments or to provide proof of data you have gathered. It is also great for comparing scenarios or the effect of one variable over another. Here I will again use the same data as used before in the table above.

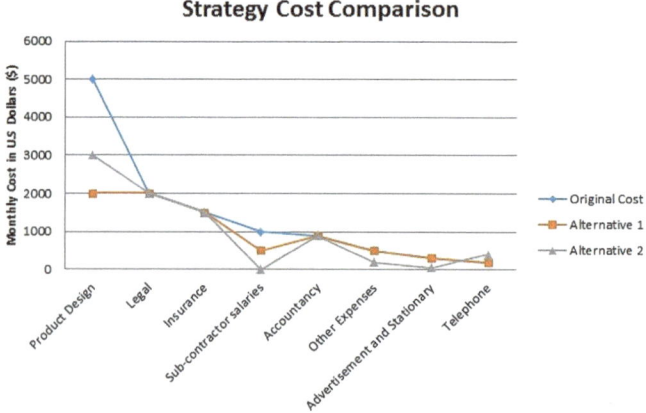

Strategy Cost Comparison

As you can see, the reader can notice at first glance that the product design for the original scenario costs more than Alternative 2.

Using visual aids is a great way to say everything you want to say but still keep the business plan short and concise.

Make It Concise

So how do we make the business plan short and concise other than taking advantage of bullet points or visual aids? The answer lies in building shorter sentences. **For example,** whenever you have a very long sentence that just does not ever seem to end and keeps going on and on continuously, it is difficult for the reader to keep track of what you are trying to say. Splitting one sentence into two will increase readability and keep the reader's attention.

It is important to use only the words you need. Writing a business plan is different than writing a novel or an book like this one. In a business plan, words like 'really' and 'very' don't serve much purpose. A good way to test your sentences is to remove a word and see if it still makes sense.

Avoid writing in more information than is needed in the main body of your business plan. Doing so may confuse or bore the reader before they even understand what your business is about. All information in the main body must be relevant to the company and easy to follow. Any additional information can go in the appendices.

Do not repeat the same information over and over again. If you have said something and backed it up, generally there is no need to revisit it. The only exception to this is if you have said something in one section that it is important for the other. You can put emphasis on it by explaining it differently as it is applied to the new concept or idea you are explaining.

Make All Relevant Information Available

Your business plan should contain all of the information you need to show or prove that you can run a successful business. Don't leave out anything important about your business. Try to leave as little to the reader's imagination as possible.

The key to writing a good business plan is to add everything that is both **relevant** and **serves the purpose of proving** that your business will succeed. Be careful about putting too much information in as the reader may not find the same value in it as you do. Select what information is important to your business and relate it to something specific in your business plan. If you cannot relate it directly to something, the information is either redundant or too generic, and must be removed.

Additionally, you need to give examples and prove your calculations, designs, or concepts in any way that you can. Of course not all of this should go to the main body of the business plan especially if you have a significant amount of relevant data or evidence. You can place the most critical ones into the main body (such as the results of calculations) and keep the rest in the appendices. Do not worry if you need to talk about information, tables, calculations, designs, or anything else that you have placed into the appendix, because you can reference them by placing the following reference note (See Appendix A).

Be Realistic, Write Optimistically

When writing a business plan, it is important that you stay realistic and optimistic with your goals and potential sales figures. Being just realistic or just optimistic can make your business plan unappealing. You need both so that you can keep your business plan on track and prevent it from becoming either **undersold** or **overhyped**.

When looking at raw data and market trends realistically, starting a business looks like a terrifying task. Many thoughts of potential failure or litigation sometimes make their way into a business plan. This creates an undersold business plan which reflects the fears of the writer instead of the information that the reader needs. **For example,** "If I could get enough profit, I can run my business for a few months but I don't know if I'll get it because the economy is bad and I don't know how to market my business well." The reader will be completely underwhelmed by the apparent lack of confidence and will likely not read any further.

The other extreme is overhyping your business plan. It is easy to write positive things about your company since you want it to be a success. The problem occurs when you start saying things that are exaggerated, not supported by evidence, or not true. **For example,** "Sales of my amazing and world defining product will outshine my competitors' sales by 1000% so by the end of the year, I won't even

have any more competitors!" This statement comes off as arrogant
and proves immediately that you have no idea what you are doing.

Typically in an overhyped business plan, exaggerated phrases
like "the next big thing", "better than company X", or "this is a truly
unique company" are quite common. These phrases, no matter how
much you want them to be true, are meant to mislead the reader and
will instantly be recognized by professionals.

To avoid underselling and overhyping, present to the reader all
information, analysis, and graphs underlining how realistically all of
this is helpful for the business. In the end, you are not just writing
this business plan for you, but for the readers, whoever they may be,
so that they may be **convinced** that your business will sustain itself
and grow. If you are not honest and confident with yourself about
your own business plan, then it gives the reader no reason to trust
you. Even when you need to talk about the risks of the company, you
should remain positive by representing the threats honestly and
clearly, but add how you will be **overcoming** these threats with
realistic arguments that the reader will believe.

What Else to Avoid

At this point, you should have a pretty good idea of what to
avoid when writing your business plan. However, there are some last
minute things I need to cover.

AVOID BEING TOO TECHNICAL

Readers will often lose focus if you throw too much
information at them at once or use terms that are specific to your
field. Remember that not everyone understands the same things that
you do. Make sure that all of the information is easy to read and
understandable. Of course if your business is related to an
engineering or other technical field, you will need to provide
important technical details. However always keep in mind who is
going to read your business plan and make sure you write it in a way
that they can understand what you are trying to convey.

BAD GRAMMAR AND SPELLING

Bad grammar and spelling is your worst nightmare. If the
reader cannot understand what you said, he or she will lose focus
quickly and not take your business plan seriously. Alternatively,

misspelt words can be very distracting and even if a reader goes through your entire business plan, he or she may not recall anything other than your atrocious spelling.

NOT LISTING RISKS

Even if you have an amazing business plan, readers will feel uneasy if you do not list the risks of your business. Listing the risks will show the reader that you understand what could happen and how you plan to deal with it.

Follow these links for more helpful information:

http://venturebeat.com/2010/11/24/17-words-not-to-use-in-a-business-plan/

http://www.caycon.com/why-business-plans-dont-get-funded.php

CHAPTER 3: PREPARATION

Whether you have previous experience in business or not, you need to prepare many things before you delve into the actual business plan. This section will give you useful resources and things to consider during the preparation stage.

This stage is when you will envision the basis of the business and make an outline of key points that you want the reader to know. If you do this stage before starting the actual business plan, you will need to update it fewer times since everything was planned out beforehand.

For preparation of your business plan, consider doing the following:

✓ Research
✓ Take Notes / Make an Outline
✓ Conduct Analysis
✓ Ready Company Assets
✓ How Long Should the Plan Be?
✓ Formatting

An important note is that if your business idea is not clear or if you are not sure if it is feasible or profitable with the information at hand, by doing what I discuss in this section, you will realize that you have not only written an impressive business plan, but have pretty much everything you need to start your business.

Research

You should be doing two types of research:

Primary Research: Primary research includes everything that you personally do to gather data. An example of this is doing market research, such as conducting a survey either online or in person. The advantage of primary research is that you have full control over the research and how you go about conducting it. That means that any data you collect will be more relevant to your business since you know what to focus on.

Secondary Research: Secondary research includes all of the information that is already available to you through all the different mediums. You can find information about the type of business you will be doing in libraries, business journals, trade associations, government websites, etc. The downside to secondary research is that any market research or study anyone else did may not completely relate to your business. When doing secondary research, it is always wise to pick reliable sources. The following resources should be helpful for your secondary research.

✓ United States Department of Commerce
✓ Bizstats.com
✓ Small Business Development Centers
✓ All Business
✓ Hoovers.com
✓ Dun & Bradstreet

Keep in mind that these are websites that might be useful for business plans as applied to all sectors. You should do a research thoroughly to find out extra information specific to your industry. Look for statistics, charts you can compare your data with. This way you may realise competitive advantages that you can underline in your business plan.

Take Notes / Make an Outline

It is always important to take notes when you are preparing to write your business plan. I prefer to take notes on paper first about each section, and then start writing the business plan section by section. However, the method in which you plan it is really up to you. In your notes, you can remain as general or get as detailed as you like.

Alternatively, you can write everything in a text editor such as Word. By taking notes electronically, you can convert your notes quickly in cohesive sentences. This can save you time provided you have a device to take notes on handy. Again, the method is entirely up to you.

If you would like to take this one step further and use numerous different features, there are plenty of free note taking software that you can download online at. Among the most popular is Evernote.

You can explore additional software here:

http://uk.pcmag.com/productivity-products/13459/feature/top-free-software-picks-note-taking-and-outliner-a

Conduct Analysis

Conduct calculations and analysis. All sections should be one way or another be based on analysis or designing proof of concepts. For example, financial statements, pricing, analysis of survey results, SWOT, risk assessment etc are examples. I will go into detail about all these within the section descriptions they belong to in Chapter 4. Unfortunately I can't give you specific examples as each business will have different needs.

Ready Company Assets

Having your company assets ready before your business begins adds a bit more credibility to your business plan. Examples of company assets that you would need to prepare are: a business logo, website domain name, business cards, letter headed paper, company invoice, price lists for services or products to be sold if you have them, proof of approved or pending patents, etc. As you can tell, there are quite a few things you need so that can be ready when your business opens its' doors. Out of all these, the business logo, price lists, and the business website (if you have it) are what you should have in the business plan. The other ones are necessary items for your business but are not critical for the purpose of writing your business plan.

You will place the business logo on the title page so it is important. You can place the price lists for your products and services in the appendix to show how much you will charge your clients or customers.

Here is a great website for a professional looking and affordable logo:

http://www.logonerds.com/

Alternatively you can make your own logo. Check out other options here:

http://homebusiness.about.com/od/Home_Business_Toolbox/tp/7-Affordable-Or-Free-Logo-Maker-Tools.htm

How Long Should The Plan Be?

The main body of the business plan, meaning everything except the appendices, should ideally be 15 to 20 pages long. This can be a challenge when you have an abundance of information, however if you apply at least some of the things I have discussed you can achieve the ideal length. The appendices can be a maximum of 20 pages by themselves. In the appendices, you can put all of the company assets and documentation related to all sections of the business plan. A good rule of thumb is if it does not add value to the business plan and/or is not referenced anywhere in the business plan, do not even put it in the appendix.

Formatting

Here are some pointers that you **must** do to make your business plan look professional and create consistency throughout the entire plan:

✓ Use a single font and only that font throughout the entire document including titles and appendices.
✓ Keep text sizes consistent such as sizes of section titles, subsection titles, etc.
✓ Keep the titles in black. Do not use colored text. However, you can use bolded, underlined, or italic text to emphasize key points, but don't overdo it. Visual aids used in the main text will have enough effect on balancing the overall monochrome feel so do not worry about adding colored text.
✓ Keep some white space on all of your pages. Do not fill it entirely with text as this can be tiring for the eye. However, do not use double spaced text either because the large spacing between the lines could distract the reader from the content. Aim for a 1.15 spacing size and organize your information into bullet points. This should help you keep some white space.
✓ These are the most important points. Other than this, as long as it is appealing and the text is properly edited, you are good to go.

CHAPTER 4: WRITING IN ACTION, SECTION BY SECTION

By now, you should have a pretty good idea of what your business is and why your business plan is so important. By now, a significant amount of information, analysis, resources, and any proof that will boost your credibility are all prepared.

All of this means that we can delve into details of the specific sections. There is no outline that is set in stone. The key things here are that you prove to the best of your ability that your business is needed by your clients (in other words, you are fulfilling a market demand), your idea is financially and logistically feasible, and you have enough credibility to show you know what you are doing.

Here is an outline that I have used and recommend:

- ✓ Title Page
- ✓ Executive Summary
- ✓ Table of Contents
- ✓ Overview of the Business
- ✓ Marketing and Selling A Product or Service
- ✓ Making and Delivering A Product or Service
- ✓ Strategy
- ✓ The Team
- ✓ Financial Analysis
- ✓ Legal Aspects and Sustainability
- ✓ References
- ✓ Appendices

In terms of which section to write first, writing the appendices first has been significantly easier for me because this way, I was able to know what I will write about. It tells me how I am going to distribute the information among sections and which aspects I will discuss or leave out. Appendices include all excel calculations, design documents, results of marketing surveys, financial forecasts, and any other related information.

The executive summary, despite it being one of the first things we are covering, should be one of the last things you do. It effectively summarizes your business so it makes more sense to write everything else in your business plan and then summarize what you wrote at the end.

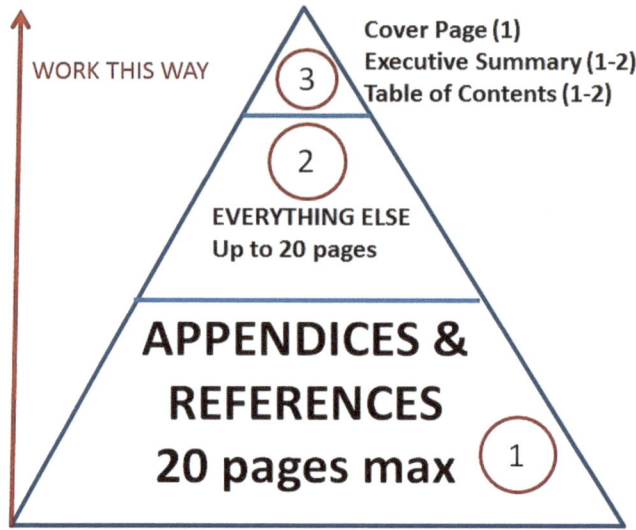

The numbers in parenthesis show how many pages the section should be. This pyramid representation should make it clear where you should start and how long the section should be.

All Right!! With all of that settled, let's go over the sections one by one, discussing everything you need to generate an impressive business plan.

Title Page

The title page should be neatly organized and appealing to the eye because this is the first page the reader sees. For this section, I will be assuming you are using Word to make your business plan as it is the program I use.

It should include the following:

✓ Logo and name of the business
✓ The month and year the business plan was written
✓ Names of partners who developed the business plan
✓ Contact information of the Chief Executive Officer or business owner
✓ A confidentiality statement

Follow these steps to create the title page, preferably using a Times New Roman or Arial font (which are both widely used for writing business plans):

Step 1: Place the company logo right under the header section. Go to the 'insert' tab, then click on the 'picture' button, and select your business logo to place it inside the document. Then click on the logo and go to 'Home' tab, and in the paragraph category click 'Center' to center the image. Resize the business logo so that it covers 2.2 inches of the page. You want the business logo to be clearly visible but not cover up too much of the page.

Step 2: Then go to the center of the document and write the following:

Business Plan for 'place business name here'.

Use a large font size (between 24 and 30 should do it) to make the name more visible. Additionally bold this title. Then, go below the title and if there are any subtitles, place them underneath the Business Plan Title with a smaller font size (between 18 and 20).

Step 3: Right below that enter the Month and Year the business plan was written with an even smaller size (about 16), in the form of month, year (January, 2015).

Step 4: At the bottom of the page, write the company address and the contact information of the CEO or whoever prepared the business plan. Contact information constitutes the address, telephone number, and e-mail of the business or if the business does not have an address yet, the information of whoever assumes the responsibility to be contacted by investors. This information should be the smallest font size (12).

Note: Another thing to keep in mind is that this page should not be covered with text. Spaces help the reader to distinguish information from one another. Play with the fonts until you are satisfied with the title page.

Here is a link for a sample Title Page:

http://www.businessplanhut.com/title-page-example-jb-incorporated-business-plan

Executive Summary

This is the heart and soul of any business plan and is where you will summarize, in an efficient manner, the most important points you have conveyed in the business plan. It should be written after all other sections are written so that the flow of facts will be improved.

The executive summary should ideally be 1 page long, however 2 pages is all acceptable if there is too much to say to fit on a single page.

You should include the following in the executive summary:

✓ Your business name, location, and what kind of a company it will be (private, limited liability, or corporation).

✓ **What** need does your business fulfill, or what problem does it solve?

✓ **How** will your business accomplish this? What is special about it?

✓ Include a summary of marketing survey results or anything that proves there is a market for your product or service.

✓ Briefly talk about key people in the management team who will accomplish all this, and how it is relevant to their background.

✓ Lay out with bullet points key figures or results from the analysis related to financing, start-up costs, revenue projections, break-even point, operational costs, etc.

✓ Wrap up with one or two sentences saying that all proof has been provided within the business plan and in the appendices sections and the business will be flexible to the reception of the service or the product by the customers and continually increase the quality of the product or service as well as customer satisfaction.

Table of Contents

The table of contents is a fairly straight forward section. Put "Table of Contents" at the top of the page and place each section header underneath it. It is recommended that you number each section header so that the reader can easily follow your business plan. As mentioned earlier, this is one of the last things you will write so don't write it first and be forced to continuously update it. It just wastes your time that could be better spent on the other sections.

For example:

Table of Contents

You can create an automated table of contents by going under 'References' Tab in Word and selecting 'Table of Contents'. Remember to right click on the table of contents that you have placed, select 'Update Field' and choose 'Entire Table'. Doing this ensures that the Table of Contents reflects the changes you have made to the business plan.

Overview

This section gives detail about what the business does. While you are writing this section, try to get as specific as you can. **For example,** instead of just saying, "We will start a Chinese restaurant", say, "Our restaurant branches will be based on the Chinese cuisine offering the only chicken foot dish within a 100 mile radius of Durham."

First, you must place your mission statement and elaborate on it. Your mission statement is what your business will do and is the driving force for why you are starting a business in the first place.

Then talk about the overall market and what kind of competitive advantages your business has. State which industry your business belongs to and explain the how the well that sector is doing. Then cover why your business is special in that sector. **For example,** "The alcohol industry in the USA generated $100 billion in revenue in 2014 and is expected to grow by another 30% in 2015. For the first time, our business will be importing a select wine from France that has won 1 national and 3 regional rewards into the state of Indiana."

However, **do not** make a statement like: "If our business can grasp 0.01% of this sector in the first year, all of our start-up and operational costs will be paid for and we will have profit left over to expand our business." Without any proof to back this up, you are just stating that the large revenue of the sector overall will keep your business afloat. Just because the sector is doing well does not mean you will be doing well. Professionals will not fall for this. However if you can prove it, you are of course free to do so.

After this, you need to show what kind of a role your business will take within the overall industry. Underline any positive aspects of your business such as quality of the service or product, affordability, etc. Since you have bought this book, you have probably been thinking about your business and have found a gap in the market or are on the road to finding one. Ask yourself the following questions, "**Why** do people **need** this product or service", "**Why** will my business **grow**?", and then explain it in this section.

Now give details about what the product (or service) is for and the demographics of what clients you expect (or have proven through market surveys) will have the highest demand for the product or service. What age group is this product for? Is it gender specific or gender neutral?

Then, go into detail about the design of the product and its' function or elaborate on the service you are offering or will be offering.

Lastly you can still put some key figures from the other sections of the business report. This is not a repetition, shorter version of for example what is explained in the financial section of the report. This is necessary because even though you should aim for everyone reading your report all the way, you should not assume that will happen. Overview, gives more detail then the executive summary however it is still a summary. Use this section well as an opportunity to provide further detail about anything that you could not fit in the executive summary, but is still very important. Remember that first impressions are extremely important so if you can **really** impress the reader by the end of this section, you will have their full attention throughout the rest of the business plan. The rest of the report is basically proof and discussion for everything you say in executive summary and overview.

Marketing and Selling A Product or Service

All proof, analysis, and discussion related to marketing the product or service goes here. The best way to prove that your product is selling is to already be selling it. However, I have assumed during most of this book that the business was not started yet, which is often the case provided you are reading this book to write a business plan.

4 P'S OF MARKETING

The 4 P's of Marketing is a guideline to help you get a clear picture of your product or service for the purpose of marketing it efficiently. You need to think about the following P's:

Product: Which product will you be offering and what customer need does it fulfil?

Price: At what price will you be offering the product or service?

Place: Where will you be offering the product or service? Have you determined the right locations for your sales operation? How will consumers buy what you offer? (online, physical store etc.)

Promotion: How will you advertise and attract consumer attention to what you are offering? What kind of strategy will you follow to achieve maximum exposure to your product or service?

CHOOSE A PRICING METHOD

First, start by calculating the price of your product or service. You could do that within the financial section as well however it is better to place it here since you are talking about selling the product. Putting an appropriate price tag on your product or service and discussing it is the first task.

You may use numerous pricing methods for your products or services:

Cost-Plus Pricing: This type of pricing is when you write down the costs for all parts within the final assembly of a product or all components needed to provide a service, and average it down to represent the cost of a single unit. Then, you increase the **average cost** by a fixed percentage (choose the best profit margin for your business) to get the price of a single unit. Profit margins differ for different businesses and industries. **For example,** within the food industry, a 30% profit margin is commonly used. To get the price for a single unit, include all costs related to the manufacturing of a product (including packaging) to ensure you have the right price and you do not incur losses. If you forget to add all of the costs, you might end up putting the wrong price tag and especially if you have a low profit margin this will spell trouble. Remember that customers do not like prices to change frequently especially to the up-side.

Differential Pricing: If you select to price your product or service this way, it means that you would price the product depending on the clients' purchasing power, quantity ordered, delivery time, and payment terms. The idea of differential pricing is to vary the pricing with respect to what the customer is willing to pay.

Marginal Cost Pricing: Using this type means pricing the product at or slightly above the variable cost to produce it. Fixed cost is cost of producing a unit that does not change with quantity produced. Variable cost does change depending on the quantity produce. This type of pricing used if the product cannot be sold for higher prices, and if there is excess inventory. The idea here is to place the lower price possible to keep the business ticking over. In some circumstances, selling the product at marginal cost pricing might be better than not selling it at all. This is not a healthy way of pricing a product however if you are not selling well and you need to compete by putting more of your product out in the market, this might be a temporary solution for you.

Market Pricing: This is when you place the same price tag on your product or your service as the widely excepted rate of the market. In other words, the rate at which your competitors are selling similar a product or service. If your product or service is new and you want to compete well, this can be a great strategy for you, especially if you have a high competitive advantage. By pricing the same level as your competitors, customers or clients will not be intimidated by your price (because they are used to paying that price) and will likely be impressed by what makes your product of service better than your competitors.

Mixed Pricing: This is when you charge a fixed rate for a base service and then hourly for additional work that needs to be done. This is similar to how many lawyers get paid. It is usually more relevant to the service industry than a product driven one. This is a good pricing strategy if you want to get a flat rate in advance and charge hourly to get more revenue depending on how long your work hours are.

Negotiable Pricing: Widely used within the construction industry, the price is changed depending on the customer specifications and what both you and your clients agree on. To do this properly, you need to have done proper research and calculations for what you are building or selling. Additionally, you need to do research on the clients and try to estimate how much they would be willing to pay. Then you can start negotiating at an even higher price and try to come to terms with what the customer is willing to pay above the costs you will incur.

Penetration Pricing: You have an exciting product or service. You are new to the market and your competitors business is widely accepted with a large client base. Do not be intimated by them as you can use a method called penetration pricing. You will set the cost by determining the lowest price you can charge to get a larger share of the market. This strategy means that you may need to incur some losses at the beginning until you get the market share that you are aiming for. Only then can you increase the price. However, people do not like random price increases so you can accomplish this with a marketing campaign when you start selling your product. Tell your customers or clients that these low prices are for a limited time only. This way you can increase the price of what you are offering without surprising your customers or clients.

Promotional Pricing: This is usually used after you have entered the market and realized that sales are not doing well. In this case, you can do the following:

Bundle Pricing: Combine various services or products together for a limited time and sell them as a bundle.

Complementary service or goods: You can say if they buy a product or use a service, a similar one is free.

Stock clearance: This is when you say, "We need to sell everything as fast as we can," and you place various levels of discounts on your products or services.

Skim Pricing: This is used by widely known businesses where high prices do not have an effect on demand. Their customers tend to be very wealthy individuals who do not care how much a product or service costs. **For example,** in very high end clothing stores, you will realize that there are no price tags on the products because the business has such high prestige that their customers buy from them just for the name alone. These businesses have little competition and that is why they can increase their prices similar to a monopoly.

FORECASTING AND MARKET RESEARCH

After you have chosen your pricing method, your next step is to discuss sales or collect marketing data so that you can create your **cash flow forecast.** A cash flow forecast is a plan that looks into the future so that you can anticipate any cash flow problems that may occur. All this entails is predicting your business revenue as well as costs. This will allow you to determine months with a negative cash balance, months with unusually costs, trends in revenue, etc. It is good to practice this now as you will be doing it often when the business gets started.

If you are already selling the product or service, you can simply place proof of how many units you are selling into the appendix and **discuss it** (with only key numbers and charts) in this section. The good news here is that you should already have lots of data about the market since you are making sales and better access to your end user. Additionally, you can talk about your plan on how to improve the marketing of the product or service and increase revenue.

If you are **not** selling the product, you should conduct market research first, put **proof of market research** in the appendices (as well as the survey questions), and discuss the results in this section. There are several ways you can do market research:

Speak to potential customers informally

Interview potential customers formally

Use an online surveying service

Speaking to potential customers informally means you can call customers and ask them whether they would buy the service or product you will be offering. There can be significant disadvantages to doing this such as no control over the demographic, risking potential customers hanging up on you before you can get any data, spending time categorizing the data, and the high costs of such an elaborate effort. If you can acquire enough data, you can approximately determine what your future sales might be.

Interviewing potential customers formally provides some advantages over interviews conducted on the phone. You can achieve this by talking to people on a busy street and trying to get their attention with visual stimulus such as fliers. This offers an advantage because the person surveyed can give more of their attention to the survey because they can physically see you or the people you have hired. Have the survey and a pen ready to save people time and decrease the likelihood that they would just take off while you are making papers ready. Alternatively, you can set up a focus group study with a local college to have a captive audience. In my opinion, formal interviews are the most accurate surveying technique because compared to the others, this provides more accurate results.

Using an online surveying service also has its' advantages as well. You can pay a website to find specific demographics (based on age group, gender, etc.) or you can supply a link to individuals yourself to complete the survey online. This is advantageous because you can reach a lot of people with little effort, without even leaving your computer. However, the results may be inaccurate as the survey takers might not read it thoroughly so that they can finish it quickly.

PREPARING A SURVEY

A survey is helpful both before and after your product or service has launched. For now, I am assuming that your business has not begun yet. When preparing a survey, consider placing a short description of your service or a picture of your product (could be physical or a CAD model rendering) at the beginning of the survey. Give information about the function of the product or the usefulness of the service. Then write your questions based on what you need to know.

Here are some sample questions and why you should ask them:

1-) Do you buy similar products (or use similar services) to this one and if so, how often?

Choices: These are simple yes and no questions but you need to follow up with "why" or "why not" every time. This will help you get a better sense of what you should focus on during advertising or what you could do to make your product more appealing. The amount of time they spend using a service or product is also useful information to know.

2-) Where would you or do you buy the product or service from? (Please choose all that apply)

Choices: List everywhere your product is sold or will be sold. If you are directly selling your product, list all of your competitors and include an "other" option so you can determine if you have any other competitors that you may not have considered.

3-) Why do you buy this product?

Choices: Make sure to include every reason you want the product to be sold or known for. This way if those options are selected, you can infer that there is high demand for your product. You also need to include some other options for the question but if you cannot, you can have the user fill in their own answer.

4-) How would you pay for this product or service?

Choices: You can use intervals in the choices such as 'between $5 to $10' for the choices. Research how much your competition is selling the product for so that none of the multiple choices here would be insignificant. This will help you understand if customers are willing to pay more for this product or not (is the demand for the product price sensitive?), and how this places your pricing with respect to your competition. Alternatively, you could have the survey taker enter in an amount but typically they won't for any number of reasons.

5-) Could the current product or service you are using be improved?

Choices: List all of the possible improvements and allow them to fill in their own answer. The improvements should be relevant to your design of product or service.

6-) How does our product or service compare?

Choices: The answers can range from 'very good' to 'very bad' but remember that since the survey takers have not had a chance to use your product or service yet, they are basing their decision on what information you provided to them.

7-) How likely is it that you would buy our product or service?

Choices: Anywhere from 'very likely" to 'not likely at all' will give you the answers you need. Since your product or service is not out yet, chances are you will get positive reviews if you showed your product off well enough.

8-) If not, how could we improve it?

Choices: This continues from the previous question. The answer for this one has to be written in as there is no way you can predict all of the potential improvements.

9-) What do you like (or like most) about our product or service?

Choices: You can write choices like good functionality, aesthetically pleasing design, low cost, high quality, great durability, etc. Whatever you feel makes your product or service special, make sure you make that an answer.

10-) How much would you expect to pay for our service or product?

Choices: While similar to question 4, this will tell you if anyone is willing to pay more or less than your competitors to use your product. Again, list ranges for the choices.

At the end of the survey, ask information about the survey taker. Include gender, age, general interest in product or service, etc. You can place your analysis of the raw data into the related appendix.

There is **A LOT** you can infer using the survey results. You can discuss your findings in the main body and make a few conclusions:

✓ There is a market demand (hopefully significant based on the results).

✓ What customers like most about your product or service (shows that you are original and you are game for the long run).

✓ What customers are willing to pay and what price you are willing to sell.

✓ What improves you can make to the product or service in the near future so it better fits your 'best customer satisfaction' policy.

✓ You are offering the **right** price. It can be a more expensive than usual but if it is special and customers are willing to pay higher prices, you do not necessarily have to offer the **cheapest** product.

✓ Your expectations of market demand (based on customer age, gender, etc.) are justified. If they are not justified, how can you adjust to this?

Please keep in mind that these are just examples and you can build your own questions depending on what *you* want to *find out*. I am only aiming to give you ideas so you can have a place to start.

PRESENTING THE SURVEY RESULTS

Make charts, tables, or plots based on your findings and try to keep the descriptions short and to the point. You do not have to put visual aids for all of the points you want to prove but you can select the ones most important to your business and put emphasis on them. The rest of the results can be put in bullet points.

Don't forget to talk about the sample size (how many people filled out the survey). The larger the audience you surveyed, the more significant your results become. Present your findings directly (by using percentages, numbers, etc.) and describe why the data is either good or bad for your marketing strategy and sales.

For example, you can say, "Based on the analysis of the survey results, 60% of the customers expected to purchase our product are within the age range of 20-25. This is in line with our initial estimation and as such we will focus our marketing efforts to increase our brand exposure among the younger generation."

Finish the entire section up by talking about the **actions** you will take based on the results. What is your marketing strategy to make the best use of your findings? You can use social media, newspapers, television, radio, or other sources for **advertising**.

By now, you have shown that you know what your customer wants **and** you have proven to others that you are in control of your business. You have removed the mystery of whether your product will sell or not and you have an **action** plan to reach out to potential clients and improve sales. You are well on your way.

Making and Delivering A Product or Service

In this section, you will explain the design aspects if you are manufacturing a product or the procedures and methodology to be followed if you are offering a service. You will also discuss how you will deliver the end result to your clients/customers such as shipping arrangements, logistics, deliverables, etc.

PRODUCT

If you are dealing with a product, all information about manufacturing goes here. This information includes:

Where is the factory going to be located? How large is it? Details about the expected production rate. Assembly requirements.

How many parts are there in the product? How will the product assembled? Are there any welding or other manufacturing operations involved? Who will assemble the product, people, robots, or both? How much precision is involved during the manufacturing process? What is the rework rate and what kind of improvements in the design has been made to minimize this? Is there going to be any field service required to maintain the units' continued operation?

In terms of distributing the products:

Packaging. Distribution costs. Choice of transportation company. How long will it take to deliver the products to different states or internationally if applicable? How will customers order the product (online payment, by asking for a quote, filling out a form, etc.)?

If you will be delivering more than 1 product, you can include a product list in the appendices and discuss which model or product will take the most time or money to produce. You can also create a Pareto chart comparing models or products.

Also you can discuss the logistics of your operations. **For example,** why you have selected the specific location for your manufacturing operations? Is it strategically located to deliver the products quickly? Does location help in getting parts from suppliers?

SERVICE

For a service, all the information about running and maintaining the service go here. This information includes:

How will the service be delivered? What are the deliverables (reports, presentations for a consulting company, etc.)? Who will be delivering the service? Who will take the calls?

For the service, you can include a flowchart in the appendices section to show how the service will be created and delivered. You can put a simplified version of this into the main body of the report and discuss it, or simply reference to the section in the appendices where you place it.

Strategy

This section covers the main strategies that will allow you and the reader to better understand your business. When you write this, it is best to organize everything in this manner:

- ✓ Overall Strategy
- ✓ SWOT Analysis
- ✓ Strategy for Expansion
- ✓ Exit Strategy

OVERALL STRATEGY

The overall strategy is where you can talk about the business in more detail. Represent and elaborate on your business' mission statement, vision, and values.

The mission statement is a chance to get customer's attention on **what your business does**. Think about what product and service you are offering and tailor it into a short sentence that will catch customer's attention. **For example,** if you are going to be developing iPhone and Android applications, your mission statement could be:

'We exist to develop functional applications for iPhone and Android devices that not only meet but exceed our client's expectations, and we will consistently deliver to our clients creative, high performance, and end user friendly applications.'

This statement explains what you are doing for your clients or customers and what principles you uphold while you are doing it. The mission statement for this specific example underlines a continuous process in which this business will deliver the best applications that generate high revenue and are likely to become popular.

Your vision will explain **what your business wants to be**. Continuing with the mobile application development business example, you might say:

'Through our innovative approach on problems and our ever increasing expertise, we thrive to become a leading application developer, and to create apps that have a genuine impact on users lives thereby boosting their quality of life.'

As you can see, you are still developing applications for your clients but you are putting emphasis on the end user. If you put this statement on your website, your direct clients will realize that you care about their success. After all, if you make the end users happy, your direct clients will be happy too since they will generate revenue and receive good feedback from the end users. You are emphasizing that you really want to make a difference in people's lives by developing the best applications that solves a problem. Of course, don't forget that if you want to make statements like these, you better be able to prove them.

Values will show **how you work.** For this part, you should direct the readers' attention to some of the core values you uphold (such as collaboration, user friendliness, customer satisfaction, passion, etc.). Whatever your values are, explain each of them with an attention grabbing sentence. You need 3 to 5 values. Below 3 is too few, above 5 is too many.

Here is an example of Values:

Passion: We are a dedicated team who is dedicated to creating an app that our clients can be proud of.

Customer Satisfaction: We strive to listen and engage with customers regularly to make sure their experience with our products is a favourable one.

Communicative: We aim to consistently update our clients on progress and never leave them in the dark.'

You can regroup mission-vision-values into a single page with a nice design to show all of them together. It is a good idea to place it into the main body but if you have more important visual aids prioritize those (such as their relation to financial analysis, the product or service, or marketing).

A stakeholder map places your business to its' center and graphically represents all stakeholders as connected to your business. Stakeholders are shown within circles and the more important they are the bigger the circles are.

Below is a simplified version of a stakeholder map:

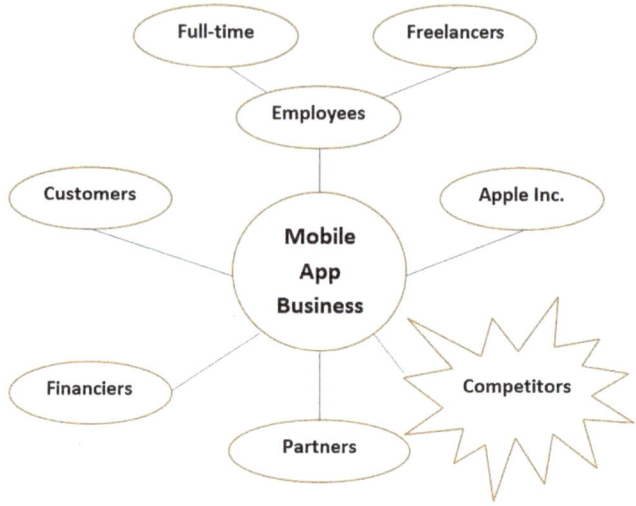

You can put more stakeholders and branch them off as you see fit to create an accurate and elaborate stakeholder map as applied to your business.

You should discuss the stakeholder map you have prepared in this section but if it takes up too much space you should stakeholder map itself into the appendix. Lastly, you can discuss your current partnerships or possible partnerships your business may form in the future.

SWOT ANALYSIS

A SWOT analysis is an analysis of the business that looks into the strengths, weaknesses, opportunities, and threats in a well organized chart.

A SWOT analysis examines the following:

Strengths: Think about the advantages your business has. What kind of resources do you have that others do not? What factors will help you sell your product or service?

Weaknesses: What should you avoid? What could you improve? What factors might reduce your sales?

Opportunities: How can you improve your product or service? What trends can you spot and take advantage of? Does the government have a policy that can benefit your business?

Threats: What challenges will your business face? What are your competitors doing and how this might affect your business? Is your company financially sound? Could there be something that can seriously threaten the existence of the business?

Here is an example of a SWOT analysis:

Strengths	Weaknesses
Qualifications	New business
Significant experience	Highly competitive
Competitive pricing & incentive schemes	No staff
Minimum outgoings & little start-up costs	App development can be hit or miss with consumer
Growing industry	
Provides services AND develops/releases apps itself to increase profits	
Low cost/high return potential	
Opportunities	**Threats**
Strategic alliances/partnerships	Strong competition/competitive pricing
Market demand	Changing economic and market trends
High volume, high quality, increased awareness =success	Price inflation/deflation
Improve product design side of the business using profits from apps or vice versa	

From here, you can discuss the important points that are worth mentioning. Underline your strengths and explain how to deal with threats.

As with all sections under Strategy, it is best to place the SWOT analysis into the appendix section and discuss the important points here. **Alternatively**, you can place a shorter version of it here so that the readers have easy access and reference the appropriate appendix for the detailed version.

STRATEGY FOR EXPANSION

The best way to write this part is to create long term and short term goals related to expansion of the business. Expansion could be in terms of how many clients you have, how many products you are selling (or your market share), how many facilities or branches you possess, starting operations in other states or internationally, etc.

First define what short term and long term is for you. **For example,** short term could be 3 months and long term could be 2 years for your business. This decision should be made by looking into other similar businesses and coming to a realistic length of time.

Some of your strategy may help to build the foundation for your long term goals. If this is the case, you can create a table that lists the short and long term goals and place the related ones next to each other. Or you can use bullet points categorizing business goals into short term and long term separately.

After you have done this, briefly discuss the most important points on **how** you are planning to achieve these goals.

EXIT STRATEGY

An exit strategy constitutes what founders or investors could do to leave their holdings (or part of the business) and ride off into the sunset. The reasons you or your investors might want to let go of the business can be as follows:

Liquidation: If the business or company is doing very well, part of the team or investors may simply want to liquidate their stake and take their cut. This is not necessarily a bad thing because the business can then take on new investors or partners. The funds generated from this may be used to further expand the business.

Business not doing well: The business may be incurring debts and may not be running as well as planned. Maybe the product or service did not sell well and resources are dwindling.

Your exit strategy can be one of the following:
- ✓ Transfer the company to a family member
- ✓ Sell the company to one or more key employees
- ✓ Sell to employees using a stock ownership plan
- ✓ Sell to one or more co-owners
- ✓ Sell to a third party
- ✓ Engage in a Public Initial Offering (if the business is privately owned or if it is a limited liability company)
- ✓ Retain ownership but turn into a passive owner
- ✓ Liquidate holdings

Please note that these choices are only for the founders, partners, or investors in the company. Revise the points above and think about who you can sell ownership to if need be. If you can get a letter from a family member stating that they can buy the ownership and attach it in the appendix, this could be a proof for an exit strategy.

Moreover, you can write about other strategies that can be used. An exit strategy does not necessarily mean you have to leave your stake of the company. Perhaps a certain product did not sell well and you need to start new operations until you can fix the situation. The more proof you have, the better this section will be.

The Team

Now you have written most of the business plan and it is time to get into a little bit more detail about who will accomplish all these amazing things you have **defined**, **elaborated**, and **backed up** with proof. Make this section as short as possible (1 page should be enough). Even though the talent in the business is extremely important, you should save up space for all the other sections by keeping this short. Even though you are the back bone of your business, readers expect to read more about the business rather than reading 5 pages about you.

Give information about the past success that members of the team have achieved or what kind of skills they have that is applicable to specific aspects of your business. What I mean by this is that when you state something about your or anyone's past, also say why what you said is a key trait, skill, or knowledge that can be applied to the business.

By doing this, you are saying, "Yes, I or we have come this far, we are excited, and our skills are sufficient to do a great job." Again, do not exaggerate but remember to put down all of your previous accomplishments. Essentially, be informative but not over the top. Write all the facts about your career that will help the business run smoothly and grow over time.

Financial Analysis

You have made it! You have come this far. Everything about the business should now make sense to you and anyone else. Now it is time to talk **MONEY!**

This section and the design of the product and service itself are the two sections that are likely to take the most amount of analysis. This section is all about research to be prepared to scour the internet and your local library.

Research anything you need to assemble the product or using subcontractors for a service. Remember to get quotes for everything. You need to take good and accurate notes of what you find so that you can present your business plan with realistic information. Afterwards, you can place all costs and potential costs on an Excel sheet. From here, you can try to reduce the costs by seeking new suppliers. While it is easy to keep cutting down costs, remember to not sacrifice too much of the quality as this can lead to you having an undesirable product or service. It is very hard to fix the opinion of unsatisfied customers and it will cost you more money compared to incurring more production or servicing costs.

Let's start with cash flow statement (or forecast). Here is a shortened version of a cash flow statement for an example business (shown for three months):

	A	B	C	D	E
		Dec-14	Jan-15	Feb-15	Total
6					
7	Revenue	$500	$700	$1,000	$2,200
8	Capital Introduced	$4,000			
9	Total Revenue	$4,500	$700	$1,000	$6,200
10					
11	Payments				
12	Telephone	$7	$7	$7	$21
13	Advertisement & Stationary	$150			$150
14	Public Liability Insurance	$530			$530
15	Apple Game Developer's License	$63			$63
16	Other Expenses	$30	$30	$30	$90
17	Travel				$0
18	Legal	$900			$900
19	Accountancy Fee & Bank Charge	$40	$40	$40	$120
20	PO Box purchase	$150			$150
21	Cost of freelancers	$400	$300	$200	$900
22	Total Expenses	$2,270	$377	$277	$2,924
23					
24					
25	Net Cash Flow	$2,230	$323	$723	$3,276
26	Opening Balance	$0	$2,230	$2,553	$0
27	Closing Balance	$2,230	$2,553	$3,276	$3,276

Step 1: First you need to write in your revenue for every month or if you did not start your business yet, you need to estimate the monthly revenue.

Additional capital (if any) also will count as revenue so add that up as well for whichever month it occurs. In my example, total revenue for 3 months is $6200.

Step 2: Write down all of your costs. Costs will vary from business to business so don't copy my example exactly. Add the costs up for each month to calculate the total monthly expenses. Then add up all of the costs from the 3 months you are examining to get the total cost during the time span. If you are doing a cash flow forecast, do at least 1 year in the future. If you are doing a cash flow statement, aim for starting 3 years ago or whenever your business was established.

Step 3: Calculate monthly net cash flow for each month using the equation:

Net Cash Flow = Total Revenue – Total Expenses.

Add up the number on the right side of my example to get total net cash flow for all months you are examining (shown in E25, namely $3276 in this case).

Step 4: The opening balance is whatever your business has at the beginning of the first month (in this case $0). Next month's opening balance is equal to last month's closing balance. **For example,** the closing balance for December 2014 is $2230 dollars which is also the opening balance for January 2015.

Voila!!! You have a cash flow statement. Now you know how your business' balance looks like (or is going to look like) at the end of every month. You know your cost distribution among months (you can use this data for visual aids in the business plan).

Now let's continue with an income statement on Excel using the same data.

	A	B	C
4	**Projected Profit and Loss Account for 3 months**		
5		$	$
6	**Sales**		$ 2,200
7			
8	**Overheads**		
9			
10	Public Liability Insurance	$ 530	
11	Telephone	$ 21	
12	Advertisement & Stationary	$ 150	
13	Apple Game Developer's License	$ 63	
14	Other Expenses	$ 90	
15	Travel	$ -	
16	Legal	$ 900	
17	Accountancy Fee & Bank Charge	$ 120	
18	PO Box purchase	$ 150	
19	Cost of Freelancers	$ 900	
20			$ 2,924
21			
22	Profit before Tax		$ -724
23	Estimated Income Tax		$ -
24	Net Profit		$ -724
25	**Montly Net Income**		$ -241.33

The row named 'Sales' is the revenue generated directly from sales ($2200) and does not include the $4000 capital introduced. The expenses incurred is represented under the 'Overheads', and is the total during 3 months for each expense category.

Profit before tax is calculated by:

Profit Before Tax = Sales – Total overheads

In the case of this example, your math will look like:

$$2200 - 2924 = -724$$

Because there is a loss incurred instead of a profit, the income tax will be zero but you can determine the income tax for the State you live in and apply it.

Net Profit = Profit before Tax – Income Tax

Monthly Net Income = Net Profit / Number of Months

The income statement gives a snapshot of what has happened or will happen financially by providing a monthly net income and taking into account the overall sales and expenses. You can then use your results to represent how much income you expect the business will make monthly and this will be a key figure in your business plan.

A balance sheet is prepared similarly but it is beyond the scope of this book. It is called a balance sheet because the assets your business or company has must be equal to its' liabilities.

If you would like to learn more about how to prepare a balance sheet, I have found this link useful:

http://www.myaccountingcourse.com/financial-statements/balance-sheet

For more information on business taxes, follow this link:

http://www.irs.gov/Businesses/Small-Businesses-&-Self-Employed/Small-Business-and-Self-Employed-Tax-Center-1

BREAKEVEN POINT

The breakeven point represents the moment when you will be making all of your start-up costs back and start putting cash in the bank. In other words, how long will it take for you to get rid of your start-up debt and start running on a positive balance?

In order to calculate this, you can use the income statement if you add your start-up costs as an expense. Then calculate the closing balance for all months you are examining and look for which month the closing balance will no longer be negative. You can report this by saying, "The break-even point is estimated to occur after the first 3 months of operations, at which time all start-up costs amounting to $50,000 will be recovered. It is expected that the business' ending balance will increase steadily after the 3rd month based on our calculations. Our aim is to keep this sustainable growth each month after the breakeven point; targeting a growth in the ending balance of at least 2% in the months that follow."

Legal Aspects and Sustainability
LEGAL ASPECTS

The legal aspects of your business or company are important to note especially if there are a lot of regulations in place for the industry your business belongs to. All industries that have a direct effect on the safety or well-being of the general public are highly regulated. Examples of this could be the catering, transportation, or medical industry.

In this section, you will lay out proof that you meet the criteria the regulatory body in question has in place for your business. If you do not provide the proof or do not meet the criteria, you **cannot** be selling the product or the service in the first place, however in this case you can explain how you plan to meet the criteria **as soon as possible**. What actions have you taken and what actions will you take in the immediate future to accomplish this? For example, maybe you need funding to start the business first. In this case, you might add to this section that you will have to wait for clearance from the regulatory body. Also include what you are planning to do meanwhile to run the business or get more funding.

RISK ASSESMENT

Risk assessment is the procedure where you weigh the risk of different problems that may occur or are occurring if you have started the business already. Risk assessment really can be placed anywhere in the business plan but it is best to put it into the Legal Aspects section. To conduct risk assessment, brainstorm common problems and assign them frequency and severity values.

For severity values, I prefer to use a scale out of 5 where 5 is severe and needs immediate resolution and 1 is negligible in the short run. For frequency values, you can use how many times the problem may occur monthly or weekly depending on your choice. Keep the same time frame when calculating for accuracy of the final risk values. After you have done these, multiply the severity of all problems with the frequency in which they occur. This is the value for risk of each problem.

Lastly, sort these values from highest to lowest, and discuss how you will solve each problem and in what time frame. The problem with the highest value needs to be resolved as soon as possible. For easy visualization, you can create a bar chart representing the risk value of all problems.

Discuss the results to show that yu are prepared to deal with these problems and how you plan to deal with them, and in what order.

ADDED PROTECTION

Make sure you know the insurance policies you are paying for or you will apply to in the future and what they cover (public liability insurance, employers liability insurance, professional indemnity insurance, etc.). If you do not have public liability insurance yet, try to get a quote from a well known insurance provider before you even start your business. This may be a tough process as insurance providers are reluctant to do this before you even have a business, however if you can get it, it increases your credibility and investors will see that a third party (the insurance company) thinks the idea will work and that the business is insurable. This will create a huge boost in the reader's confidence in your business.

To explore insurance plans further, follow this link:

http://www.moneysupermarket.com/c/business-insurance/public-liability/

Does the company or business have a lawyer? If yes, name the lawyer (or lawyers) and add a short description of their background. If not, figure out who will the business or company hire in the future (again, get a quote). Whether you started the business or not, the more quotes you can get, the easier and more accurate your information will be in this section.

How likely is it that the business will be sued? What kind of preventive action have you taken to minimize this possibility? How risky is the business?

If you think about these points and give information and proof about them, the investors or banks that will loan you money will see that you have considered all legal aspects and you obey the law as well as decrease the chance of the business incurring huge compensation payments if something goes wrong (hence the necessity for insurance policies).

Put any contracts and patents related to the business into this section. Providing this information will show the reader that are serious about starting this business and have already laid the groundwork to begin.

Try to make this section as short as possible by simply giving out basic information. Talk briefly about your lawyers and their general experience. Also cover your (potential) insurance policies and their general coverage as well as costs. Aim for about half a page of content if the regulations in your industry are not strict. Otherwise, try to aim for about 1 page if you can.

SUSTAINABILITY

This is a sub-section that is becoming increasingly important since regulations related to the environment and sustainability are continuously being set in place. Show that you care about the environment by placing carbon emission estimations or data inside your business plan. Is the product you are selling recyclable? Are there any regulations you need to adhere to and how you have or will achieve this? If you have test protocols, results, or design of the experiments you will conduct, you can add those as proof here.

If your business is offering a service or if it has a minimal impact on the environment, you may not need a separate section for this. Simply explain with a short sentence why you do not need to worry about it.

References

Place any reference you have acquired and used inside the main body of the report here. Additionally, if you will be buying parts online, put links to the suppliers here to prove your financial analysis. The purpose of this section is to ensure that if the reader wants to verify anything that you are saying, they **can** easily by referring to this section.

Here is a link to the MLA Referencing Guide to the Online Writing Lab (OWL) of Purdue University. Hail Purdue!!!

https://owl.english.purdue.edu/owl/resource/747/05/

This site has everything you need to get your references in the proper format. A couple of things to note is that if you are using the exact text from a source, always remember to put them in quotes on the text and give them a reference number. The reader can then verify the information in the main body by locating the matching number in this section.

Appendices

All the analysis that you used to write the business plan and other supporting information goes here. I have gone through this information throughout the entire book however let me summarize everything that can go to appendices section so you can see it all together:

Title Page (Not Applicable)

Executive Summary (Not Applicable)

Table of Contents (Not Applicable)

Overview of the Business

Business logo, product pictures and/or specifications, illustrations of what the product does and does better, any further evidence that may prove your claims

Marketing and Selling Product or Service

Pricing method choice and price calculations, survey questions, survey results and analysis (including important pie charts, bar charts, tables, etc.)

Making and Delivering Product or Service

Drawings, Manufacturing or Servicing Procedures, Organisational or Manufacturing Flow Charts, Proof of Optimization of logistics, Comparison tables for shipping costs

Strategy

Mission-vision-values, SWOT, Stakeholder map, further proof of competitive advantages, flow chart for strategy decision making (expansion and exit strategies)

The Team

Awards the management have received if any, proof related to skills, experience

Financial Analysis

Cash flow statement, Income Statement, Balance Sheet, Breakeven analysis, Start-up Costs, Financial Scenarios Comparison, showing you know why you need the money you are asking for

Legal Aspects and Sustainability

Patents, Contract with lawyers

References (Not Applicable)

Appendices (That is where we are right now)

Some tips for this section are:

✓ Again keep the formatting of everything the same as it is in the main body. You can combine appendices or reference them section by section. I prefer to have a separate appendix for each section. The title of first the appendix could be APPENDIX A: Overview of the business, for example.

✓ If you are taking screenshots of documents or placing tables or calculations from Excel, make sure the numbers are legible and key numbers are marked or underlined so that the reader can see them right away.

✓ You should now have the game plan on how to write and what you should put into your business plan. The notes you have taken will guide you through where all of your information is going to go. Idea after idea, argument after argument, proof after proof, everything will come together. It is time for you to begin writing if you haven't already.

CHAPTER 5: CONCLUSION

I wrote this book to give you ideas and a guide on how to write an impressive business plan. This is certainly a **challenging** task and even creating the appendices alone can be daunting. However, if you go through and apply all the information I have given you in this book, you will have a much better grasp of your current or future business. It is far better to have all the information about your business in one document because you will not only understand the individual sections I have described, but also the **interaction** with them as a whole. Needless to say, a well written business plan will impress readers and possibly get you the funding you need from angel investors, venture capitalists, banks, or through any other means.

Writing a business plan is a very detailed process, which I have tried to simplify for you here. Even after removing complexities, this book turned out to be longer than I expected. Keep in mind what I just said as simple and short are what you need for your business plan.

You need to say everything relevant about the business but remember, you need to ideally aim for keeping the _main body_ of the business plan less than 20 pages.

Remember that appendices are a great place to put tables, calculations, drawings, and anything that is very important but would just too take too much space in the main body. Always think about whether what you place in the main body contributes to the **flow** of the text or **strengthens** the reader's belief of your business' successful future.

I wish you success in your business endeavours and am hoping this book has been useful to you when you write your business plan. I bid you farewell until next time, by saying you should remember to:

PROVE EVERYTHING YOU CAN IN YOUR BUSINESS PLAN!!!

Other books by Mete Can Yumru

Business

Idea Generation: How to Generate Sustainable Ideas that Make Money for Your Start-up Company or Business

Trading and Investing

Dream for Pennies: 25 Tips for Penny Stock Traders

www.ingramcontent.com/pod-product-compliance
Lightning Source LLC
Chambersburg PA
CBHW040851180526
45159CB00001B/391